ACORN PANCAKES, DANDELION SALAD AND 38 OTHER Wild RECIPES

• • • •

JEAN CRAIGHEAD GEORGE

Illustrated by Paul Mirocha

HarperCollins*Publishers*

To my brothers, Frank and John Craighead
—J.C.G

To Nancy Moran for her help and support
—P.M.

Many of the recipes in this book were originally published in
The Wild, Wild Cookbook: A Guide for Young Wild-Food Foragers
by Jean Craighead George and illustrated by Walter Kessell,
Thomas Y. Crowell Junior Books, copyright © 1982 by Jean Craighead George.

The illustrations in this book were painted with gouache and colored pencil on Arches hot press paper.

Acorn Pancakes, Dandelion Salad and 38 Other Wild Recipes
Text copyright © 1982, 1995 by Jean Craighead George
Illustrations copyright © 1995 by Paul Mirocha
For information address HarperCollins Children's Books, a division of HarperCollins Publishers,
10 East 53rd Street, New York, NY 10022.

• • • •

Library of Congress Cataloging-in-Publication Data
George, Jean Craighead, date
   Acorn pancakes, dandelion salad and 38 other wild recipes / Jean Craighead George ; illustrated by
Paul Mirocha.—[New ed.]
      p.   cm.
   New ed. of: The wild, wild cookbook, © 1982.
   Includes index.
   Summary: A field guide and cookbook for finding, harvesting, and cooking wild plants.
   ISBN 0-06-021549-6. — ISBN 0-06-021550-X (lib. bdg.)
   1. Cookery (Wild foods)—Juvenile literature.   2. Wild plants, Edible—Juvenile literature.   [1. Wild
plants, Edible.   2. Cookery—Wild foods.]   I. Mirocha, Paul, ill.   II. George, Jean Craighead, date—
Wild, wild cookbook.   III. Title.
TX823.G45   1995   93-42490
641.6—dc20   CIP
                                                                                                         AC

• • • •

Book designed by Christine Kettner
1   2   3   4   5   6   7   8   9   10
❖
New Edition

CONTENTS

COME ON OUT AND GATHER WILD FOODS

When the flicker returns to my lawn in spring and the flowers of the shadbush shine like frost in the dark woodland, I am reminded that it is time to whip up a batch of dandelion fritters or a fiddlehead pie. It is April, and another foraging season has begun.

All that is needed is a penknife, a bag, and fingers. Wear old clothes and old shoes. Wild crops are found along roadsides and waterways; in marshes, fields, forests, city parks; and even on sidewalks.

I am the third of four generations of wild-food gatherers who take to the hills and fields in spring, summer, and autumn to harvest the free-growing plants, prepare them, and eat them. Grandfather taught my father, my father taught me, and I taught my children where to go for wild strawberries, fern fronds, and lamb's-quarters.

The food is fresh and healthful, but there is also the serendipity of harvesting wild foods. Unsought gifts abound. You learn the names of plants, and the birds and beasts that live with them. You discover wondrous habitats: cool waterfalls and fern-luminous groves. You might see the northern oriole pulling threads from a grapevine to weave a hanging basket nest, or a white-footed deer mouse looking up at you with huge black eyes from her nest of grasses. The greatest unsought gift is that you become aware of the interdependency of plant, bird, beast, and human.

Before you start out the back door to reap wild plants, it is important that you know how to identify them. If possible, go with a knowledgeable parent, teacher, or naturalist. Verify every plant. If in doubt, do not eat it.

Of the more than 25,000 plant species in North America, only a few are poisonous, and most of these are mushrooms. So mushrooms I pass by without exception. Most leafy plants are safe to eat, but not all. Learn the poisonous plants so you can avoid them. Learn deadly nightshade, poison sumac, poison ivy and oak, poison hemlock, and, in the west, the death camas.

Begin foraging by gathering only the plants you know. The dandelion is the best one to start with. Most of us learned the dandelion along with our ABC's. Other easily recognized plants that are edible are violets, cacti, garlic, and wood sorrel.

Learn your plants and then go foraging. There is nothing more satisfying than bringing home a wild food for the table. You feel free and independent.

—Jean Craighead George

ACORNS
· · · ·

THE OAK TREES *of the United States and Canada are varied. They all have acorns, which makes them easy to identify in autumn. Some acorns are more bitter than others, so it is best to learn the trees that produce sweet acorns. This will save you boiling and reboiling to rid them of tannin. The white oaks that grow all across the country have the sweetest acorns. The leaves of these trees do not have little sharp hairs on the ends of each leaf lobe. The red oaks do. The acorns of the white oaks need little boiling to remove the bitter taste. Gambel oak in the Rocky Mountains and the swamp white oak in the eastern United States and Canada are favorites. If your oak tree does not seem to have many acorns, remember that all nut trees have bountiful years and lean years.*

To prepare, boil acorns in a pot of water and snap off outer coats. Boil again several times, or until water comes clear. Roast in 200°F oven until nutlike and brittle. Eat as a snack or put through a coffee grinder and make acorn flour. Recipes for cooking with acorn flour follow.

ACORN PANCAKES

⅓ cup white flour

1 cup acorn flour

2½ teaspoons baking powder

¾ teaspoon salt

1 egg, well beaten

1¼ cups milk

3 tablespoons butter

In a bowl mix flours, baking powder, and salt. In another bowl mix egg, milk, and butter. Pour milk mixture into dry ingredients and stir just enough to moisten dry ingredients. Spoon onto greased hot grill or frying skillet. Flip and turn once.

Serve with maple syrup or wild jellies.

ACORN BREAD

Preheat oven: 350°F

1 cup acorn flour	1 egg
½ cup cornmeal	½ cup honey
½ cup whole wheat flour	3 tablespoons cooking oil
1 teaspoon salt	1 cup milk
1 tablespoon baking powder	

Combine acorn flour, cornmeal, whole wheat flour, salt, and baking powder. Combine egg, honey, oil, and milk. Add to dry ingredients, mixing a bit at a time. Pour into greased pan and bake in 350°F oven 20 or 30 minutes, or until a toothpick inserted comes out clean.

BERRIES

●●●●

STRAWBERRIES

Wild strawberries are first in the hearts of foragers. There is no taste that can compare with a sun-ripened wild strawberry. They grow in fields and open areas all over northeastern and north-central North America. The flowers are white. They are not to be confused with Indian strawberry, whose flowers are yellow and whose fruits are a bright, glistening red and tasteless.

RASPBERRIES AND BLACKBERRIES

Called prickly brambles by botanists, these members of the rose family produce those luscious fruits: red and black raspberries, bristly dewberry, prickly dewberry, and blackberry.

MANZANITAS

These evergreens of the Pacific coast grow on dry ridges from the lowlands to the mountaintops. The fruits can be eaten raw or in pies, the seeds ground into mush.

CURRANTS AND GOOSEBERRIES

Search for currants in lowland woods and bogs, and gooseberries in open woods, usually in and around pine forests in both the eastern and western United States and Canada.

ELDERBERRY

This shrub, three to fifteen feet tall, grows in the east and west. Look for the clustered white flowers or shining purple-black berries. It grows along washes and streams and in the soil around road culverts.

BERRY LEATHER

(Wonderful!)

Take thoroughly ripe strawberries, raspberries, or blackberries and mash to a pulp. Press through sieve to remove seeds. Spread on cookie sheet and dry in sun or oven. When dry, dust with powdered sugar and roll like a jelly roll. Store in tin boxes and jars and use as a candy treat or for pies, sauces, and tarts.

DRIED BERRIES

Spread berries on cookie sheet and put in moderate oven (325°F) until dry or place in the sun. Watch out for birds.

BERRY MILK PUNCH

½ cup wild berry juice
juice from ½ lemon
sugar or honey to taste

1 quart milk
nutmeg

Add first three ingredients to milk and serve sprinkled with nutmeg.

DIVINE BERRY TART

Preheat oven: 350°F

WILD BERRY CRUST

1 cup flour	grated lemon rind
½ cup butter	1 egg yolk

Mix flour, butter, rind, and egg yolk with hand until creamy. Roll into a ball. Refrigerate and chill about an hour. Put dough on floured board and roll flat. Place crust in pie plate.

WILD BERRY FILLING

¾ cup sugar	3 cups wild berries
½ teaspoon cinnamon	2 tablespoons butter
juice from ½ lemon	

In bowl, mix sugar, cinnamon, and lemon juice. Place wild berries in piecrust. Pour sugar mix over fruit. Dot with butter. Bake in a 350°F oven 30 to 40 minutes or until crust is brown.

CACTUS FAMILY

• • • •

CHOLLA

THIS BRIGHTLY FLOWERED CACTUS *of the southwest, also known as jumping cactus, is found in the desert above 4,000 feet. The flower buds are delicious before they open in April and May. The fruits ripen in late summer. To dethorn them, fill one of two saucepans with washed gravel and add the cholla buds or fruits. Pour from one pan to the other until thorns are banged off—four or five tosses. Pick off stubborn thorns with tweezers. Wash and boil for 15 minutes.*

PRICKLY PEAR

SOMETIMES CALLED *"beaver tail" because of its flat, round pads— tasty and nourishing any time of year—this cactus is found in the desert throughout the west, and in wastelands in the east and north- east. Large, waxy flowers appear in spring, followed by savory red fruits in summer. Bite into the sun-warmed fruit for a treat. The darker the fruit, the riper and juicier. Gather fruits with gloves or tongs to avoid spines. To clean spines from prickly pears, use a tough pair of work gloves and rub the spines off under running water.*

CHOLLA BUDS AND DANDELION GREENS

½ cup cholla buds, dethorned   2 cups dandelion greens
1 strip crisp bacon

Place cholla buds in boiling water in a saucepan and simmer for 15 minutes. Remove, pat dry, and slice. Sauté in fat from bacon strip. Boil dandelion greens for 20 minutes and drain. Place on crisp cholla buds and bacon.

CHOLLA ADE

2 cups cholla fruit, dethorned   sugar or honey
1½ cups boiling water

Cook the cholla fruit in the water until soft. Strain the juice through a colander or cheesecloth jelly bag. Add sugar or honey to taste.

CHOLLA JELLY
(Also good for other berries and fruits.)

cholla ade prepared as on page 16
paraffin

¾ cup sugar for each cup of
cholla ade

Bring the juice to a boil, add the sugar, and stir until dissolved. Cook rapidly for 5 minutes or until two drops form on the edge of a metal spoon and drop off as one. Pour the jelly into sterile glasses, cool, and cover with paraffin wax.

PRICKLY PEAR JELLY ROLL
(This recipe can also be used with jelly from any wild fruit.)

Preheat oven: 400°F

2 cups biscuit mix

⅔ cup water

1 cup prickly pear jelly,
prepared as above

Pour biscuit mix into a bowl and add water. Stir until well mixed and easy to handle. If sticky, add more mix. Turn onto floured table or board. Roll to about ½" thickness. Spread prickly pear jelly on biscuit batter. Roll lightly into loose roll. Bake in preheated oven for 10 to 15 minutes or until brown. Slice and serve with herbal tea from your area.

FRIED PRICKLY PEAR PADS

Preheat oven: 375°F

1 egg

dash of salt and pepper

½ cup cornmeal

1 cup baked prickly pear strips

½ cup cooking oil

small piece of bread

salsa (optional)

Using gloves, gather prickly pear pads. Put in aluminum foil, sprinkle with water, wrap, and bake in oven for one hour. Cut into strips.

Beat egg in a small bowl and add salt and pepper. Pour cornmeal onto a platter. Dip prickly pear strips in egg and roll in cornmeal.

Heat oil until it browns a small piece of bread, remove bread, and put prickly pear strips in pan. Cook until brown. Serve hot. Garnish with salsa (optional).

PRICKLY PEAR OMELET

2 tablespoons chopped onion

1 tablespoon oil or butter

2 tablespoons boiled, diced
  prickly pear pads

4 eggs, beaten

1 tablespoon water

salt and pepper

Fry onions in butter until transparent. Stir in prickly pear pads. Beat together eggs, water, salt, and pepper. Pour onto onions and pads and scramble quickly. Let bottom fry until brown. Fold over and serve. Don't overcook.

PRICKLY PEAR JUICE

Bring a large saucepan of water to a boil. Add 2 or 3 cups of fruit and cook for 15 minutes. Remove from water and cool.

Slice pears in half and remove seeds with thumb. Put fruit in one bowl and seeds in another.

Mash the fruit with a potato masher or food processor and strain through a colander or cheesecloth. The juice can be used to make jelly (see cholla jelly recipe, p. 17) or sweetened for punch.

Fry the seeds in butter for a crackling, nutty snack.

CATTAILS
· · · ·

CATTAILS, *those strap-leafed wetland plants with hot-dog-shaped fruits, grow over most of the United States except Alaska. When the azaleas are blooming, the emerging leaf spikes of the cattail are tender and sweet. They can be eaten raw in a salad, or cooked. In late spring the green flower spikes appear on stems much more slender than the leaf stems. The spikes are as delicious as corn on the cob and taste like it. The pollen from the male flower appears several days later about one inch above the female flower. It is rich in protein and is savory in breads, pancakes, and soups.*

The roots of the cattail, called rhizomes, are ropelike structures that grow laterally. They are delicious. Get into your old sneakers and wade into a cattail marsh. Run your hand down the leaves to the rhizomes, move along one, and pull. Wash the root, slice, and bake in the oven or boil in a pot. You cannot starve with cattails around you. An acre of cattails produces ten times as much food as an acre of potatoes.

CATTAIL LEAF SPIKES

Scrub spikes and peel to uncover the crisp whitish-green core, usually 1 foot to 18 inches long. Slice core raw into salads or boil in salt water about 15 minutes and serve as a vegetable with butter and salt.

INDIAN CATTAIL SPOON BREAD

(This moist bread is traditionally served with a spoon.)

Preheat oven: 400°F

½ cup butter	½ cup diced green pepper
2 cups fresh flower buds or cattails on the cob	salt
½ cup diced onions	1 cup sharp cheese
	pinch of chili powder

Melt butter in skillet and add cattail buds, onions, green pepper, and salt. Sauté for 5 minutes or until tender. Pour into greased baking dish. Sprinkle with cheese and chili powder. Bake until cheese melts. Spoon onto plate while hot.

CAT-O'-NINE-TAILS PANCAKES

(Shake bright-yellow pollen into a plastic bag while out in the marsh.
A dozen flower stalks will yield about a cup.)

1 cup cattail pollen

1 cup white flour

2½ teaspoons baking soda

¾ teaspoon salt

1 egg, well beaten

1¼ cups milk

3 tablespoons vegetable oil

Mix cattail pollen, flour, baking soda, and salt. Stir in egg, milk, and oil. Set aside until batter thickens, about 10 minutes. Pour daubs onto buttered skillet and fry until golden brown. Serve with maple syrup or wild jam.

CHICORY

• • • •

CHICORY'S BLUE FLOWERS, *one of the few blue flowers in nature, are transparent, round, and dazzling. They decorate roadsides and abandoned fields all over North America. The flowers have no stalks— they just erupt from the stem. Each petal is square tipped and fringed. The flowers open at sunup and are closed by noon. The bottom leaves lie against the ground and look like dandelion leaves. Chicory is also called wild lettuce. The roots can be baked in a 200°F oven, ground, and made into a substitute for strong, good coffee.*

MEXICAN GREEN SPOON BREAD

Preheat oven: 400°F

1-pound can cream-style corn

¾ cup melted butter,
    bacon fat, or chicken fat

3 large eggs

¾ cup milk

1 cup cornmeal

½ teaspoon baking soda

1 teaspoon salt

1 cup grated cheddar cheese

1 medium onion, chopped

½ cup boiled chopped
    chicory or dandelion
    greens

In a large bowl, combine the corn, butter, eggs, and milk.

In another bowl, blend together the cornmeal, baking soda, and salt. Stir dry ingredients into liquid mixture a bit at a time and blend well.

Put half the batter into a greased 9"-square pan. On top of batter put half the grated cheese, onions, and cooked chopped chicory. Pour rest of batter over this. Top with the remaining cheese, onions, and chicory.

Bake in a 400°F oven for 45 minutes or until brown. Cool slightly before spooning.

CHICORY SANDWICH

4 cups water

1½ cups washed
   chicory leaves

4 strips bacon, diced

3 tablespoons lemon juice
   or vinegar

2 teaspoons sugar

6 slices toasted bread

¼ cup grated cheese of
   your choice

In saucepan, bring water to a boil. Add chicory and simmer for 5 minutes. Drain off water.

Fry bacon in skillet until crisp. Leaving the fat in the skillet, remove the bacon and drain on paper towel.

Add chicory to bacon fat and stir-fry for 10 minutes.

Add lemon juice or vinegar. Stir. Add sugar. Stir. Cook and stir for 3 minutes over low heat. Spread onto 3 pieces of toast. Sprinkle with cheese. Set under broiler and brown, or make a sandwich and fry on griddle or skillet until golden brown. Turn once.

DANDELIONS

• • • •

EVERYONE KNOWS THE DANDELION. *The bright-yellow flowers—made up of a hundred or more little flowers, or florets, on a single hollow stem—are unmistakable. The common dandelion grows all over the United States and Canada in open, moist places, digging its long taproot down into lawns, gardens, and roadsides.*

The dandelion is one of the most useful and abundant of the wild food plants. It was brought from Europe to New England by the first immigrants and was spread all over the west through grass seed and bird droppings. This persistent species sustained many a homesteader and pioneer.

DANDELION FRITTERS

1 cup biscuit mix

1 cup milk

1 tablespoon sugar or honey

½ inch oil in skillet

4 cups dandelion flower heads
   without stems

Mix together the biscuit mix, milk, and sugar or honey. Heat oil in skillet until it sizzles when a bit of batter is dropped into it. Dip dandelion flowers into mix and drop into hot oil headfirst. Fry until golden brown. Turn with tongs and brown other side. Drain on paper towel and serve hot or cold.

WILTED DANDELION SALAD

(This wonderful salad can be made all spring and summer
if you choose the tender center leaves.)

4 cups dandelion leaves	¼ teaspoon dry mustard
4 strips of bacon, diced	salt
2 tablespoons sugar	pepper
3 tablespoons cider vinegar	2 hard-boiled eggs, sliced

Wash dandelion leaves in colander, pat dry, and place in salad bowl.

Fry bacon in pan until crisp. Remove bacon and drain on paper towels. To bacon fat add sugar, cider vinegar, dry mustard, salt, and pepper. Heat until sugar has dissolved. Pour over dandelion greens. Add crisp bacon and toss well. Garnish the salad with sliced hard-boiled eggs. Serve hot.

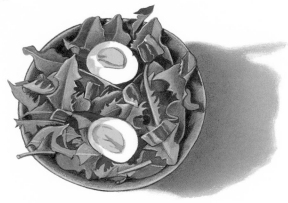

DAY LILIES

• • • •

THE DAY LILY *is unmistakable with its slender green leaf and upward-facing orange or yellow flowers. The flowers have six petals and are clustered at the top of a naked stalk. They last but one day, opening with the sun and closing at dark. Day lilies grow along roadsides and in moist wastelands. The buds, flowers, and roots are all good to eat, and are considered delicacies in Japan and China.*

WEEDY LAWN SALAD

(This is a favorite in my family. When everyone knows the weeds in the yard, young and old can contribute.)

1 cup tender dandelion greens

¼ cup each of common plantain, violet, chicory, purslane, and oxalis leaves

½ cup favorite cheese (Swiss in my house), cut into strips

½ cup boiled ham, cut into strips

2 hard-boiled eggs, sliced

1 tablespoon chopped wild garlic tops

3 tablespoons vegetable oil

1 tablespoon cider vinegar

½ teaspoon salt

¼ cup of violet, forsythia, day lily, or rose petals

Wash greens and pat dry. Place in salad bowl and mix. Add cheese, ham, hard-boiled eggs, and garlic tops. Add oil and toss.

Add vinegar and salt and toss.

Garnish with violet, forsythia, day lily, or rose petals.

LEMON DAY LILIES

2 dozen day lily buds or flowers
4 cups water
¾ cup sugar
½ cup white vinegar
1 cup canned chicken broth

1 lemon, juice and grated rind
1 tablespoon cornstarch
2 tablespoons water
2 cups cooked rice

Boil day lilies in 4 cups water for 15 minutes. Drain and set aside.

Pour sugar and vinegar into saucepan. Heat until sugar is dissolved.

Add chicken broth. Stir. Add lemon juice and grated rind. Simmer 15 minutes. Dissolve cornstarch in 2 tablespoons water. Add to sauce.

Stir until cornstarch clears and sauce is thickened.

Add day lilies and serve over rice.

FIDDLEHEADS

• • • •

IN THE SPRING OF THE YEAR, *the curled leaf buds of ferns, called fiddleheads, can be made into exotic dishes. Ferns grow everywhere except the desert and need very few words to describe them—many lacy leaflets on a branch with brown fruit dots on the underside of the frond. There are more than sixty species in the United States. The tastiest are the wood, interrupted, marsh, New York, and bracken ferns, but all are good. The bracken fern grows in the full sun in old pastures, dry roadsides, and woods over most of North America and is the favorite because it produces fiddleheads all season.*

FRIED FIDDLEHEADS

1 cup fiddleheads

2 pots boiling water

2 tablespoons butter or margarine

salt and pepper

Bring a 3-quart saucepan of water to a boil and simmer fiddleheads for 15 minutes. Drain and repeat.

Melt butter or margarine in a frying pan and sauté fiddleheads until they are brown and tender. Add salt and pepper to taste.

FIDDLEHEAD PIE

(Dandelion leaves and Jerusalem artichokes can be added.)

Preheat oven: 450°F

1 pie shell	2 chicken bouillon cubes
1 cup fiddleheads	¼ cup boiling water
2 pots boiling water	½ cup grated Swiss cheese
2 tablespoons butter	salt and pepper
2 tablespoons flour	¼ cup Parmesan cheese
¾ cup milk	3 hard-boiled eggs, sliced

Bake pie shell at 450°F for 5 minutes or until pale brown.

Remove from oven and turn heat to 350°F.

Wash and drain fiddleheads, cover with water, and boil for 10 minutes. Drain well and boil again.

Melt butter slowly in saucepan, add flour, and stir until well mixed. Slowly add milk. Keep stirring until sauce has thickened.

Dissolve bouillon cubes in ¼ cup of boiling water. Add to sauce.

Stir in grated Swiss cheese, salt, and pepper. Lightly stir in drained fiddleheads. Pour mix into baked pie shell. Sprinkle Parmesan cheese over top. Bake in 350°F oven until brown. Decorate with hard-boiled eggs. Serve hot.

JERUSALEM ARTICHOKES

• • • •

THIS PLANT IS NOT AN ARTICHOKE, *nor is it related in any way to Jerusalem. The popular name is a mispronunciation of the Spanish word "girasol," meaning sunflower. The bright, perky sunflower of central North America blooms in late August and September. Its sweet, moist tubers grow underground and are available all year round. Dig up the roundish tubers with a trowel. It seeks moist soil, stream sides, and fence rows that are in the open. Seeds can be bought from seed catalogues and planted in gardens all over the United States and southern Canada. They are attractive as well as tasty. A single plant can yield as many as twenty tubers.*

MASHED JERUSALEM ARTICHOKES

12 to 15 Jerusalem artichoke tubers

1½ quarts water

¼ cup milk

butter

salt

Scrub tubers with a stiff vegetable brush, peel like a potato, and quarter. Bring water to a boil and add tubers. Simmer for 25 minutes or until soft when poked with a fork. Drain.

Mash with milk, butter, and salt. Serve hot.

BAKED JERUSALEM ARTICHOKES

Preheat oven: 375°F

Scrub tubers, place on cookie sheet, and put in preheated oven. Bake 40 minutes or until soft. Split open and serve with butter, salt, and pepper.

OTHER RECIPES

JERUSALEM ARTICHOKES were a favorite source of starch for the American Indian. They are delicious raw in salads and excellent in fiddlehead pie. They are by far the most tasty when wrapped in corn husks and baked in a rock oven in the ground. A rock oven can be made by digging a 3'-square hole 1½' deep in the earth. Line with rocks and build a fire on the rocks. When the stones sizzle when water is dropped on them, remove coals from the fire with a shovel. Line the pit with a bed of moistened green grasses or corn husks. Season tubers with salt and wrap in corn husks. Other vegetables can be combined with Jerusalem artichokes. Nothing tastes better than a turkey or chicken wrapped in husks or aluminum foil and cooked in a rock oven. Cover with moist leaves or grass and earth. Allow 1 hour for artichoke tubers, and 2 to 3 hours for a turkey.

LAMB'S-QUARTERS

• • • •

LOOK FOR THE DIAMOND-SHAPED LEAVES *of lamb's-quarters. Some say they are shaped like a leg of lamb, and others say a goose foot. The leaves are green-blue on top, with a floury white coating on top and bottom. The plant can grow to be six or eight feet tall, and is often tinted with red in the late summer. It grows along roadsides, in fields, and in wastelands all over the United States and southern Canada. Gather June through September.*

The seeds are eaten by many birds and should be collected for your feeder. Nearly 75,000 seeds have been counted on a single plant. The Navajos use the seeds for bread and pancakes. They dry them in an oven at low heat (200°F) until crisp, then pound them into a flour. Delicious added to oatmeal as a breakfast cereal.

LAMB'S-QUARTER QUICHE

Preheat oven: 450°F

1 9" piecrust

4 strips bacon

1 onion, thin sliced

1 cup Swiss cheese, cubed

¼ cup grated Parmesan cheese

1 cup boiled, chopped
   lamb's-quarter leaves
   (dandelion, chicory, or oxalis
   can be substituted)

4 eggs, slightly beaten

2 cups cream

¼ teaspoon nutmeg

½ teaspoon salt

¼ teaspoon white pepper

Bake piecrust 5 minutes in 450°F oven. Place crust on cookie sheet. Cook bacon until crisp; remove bacon from skillet and drain on paper towels.

Cook onion in bacon fat until transparent. Place onion, cheeses, and cooked lamb's-quarter leaves in piecrust. Add crumbled bacon.

Combine eggs, cream, nutmeg, salt, and pepper. Beat with egg-beater. Pour into piecrust. Bake 15 minutes at 450°F. Bake about 10 minutes more at 350°F, until a knife inserted 1 inch from pastry edge comes out clean.

SWEET-AND-SOUR LAMB'S-QUARTERS

2 strips bacon

1 cup minced chives or onions

1 tablespoon flour

6 cups uncooked
    lamb's-quarter leaves

½ cup water

¼ cup cider vinegar

2 teaspoons sugar

1 teaspoon salt

pepper

Fry bacon in skillet until crisp. Drain on paper towels.

Cook chives or onions in bacon fat about 5 minutes. Stir in flour to make a paste.

Simmer lamb's-quarters 10 minutes in saucepan with water. Drain into bowl through colander and save liquid. In the same saucepan combine liquid from greens with vinegar, sugar, salt, and pepper. Heat over medium heat.

Add onion-and-flour mix and stir. Add lamb's-quarters and stir until mixture thickens. Cook 2 more minutes. Place in serving dish. Crumble bacon on top.

NUTS

. . . .

BLACK WALNUT

This aromatic tree with its scaly bark is found all over the eastern and central United States and Canada and out across Texas to the edge of the dry lands. A subspecies grows in California. Gather the nuts in October while they are still green and keep outdoors in a basket until the husks blacken. Knock off the husks with a hammer and crack open the savory black walnut.

SHAGBARK HICKORY

The bark of this tall tree is outstandingly shaggy. You can't miss it. Gather the egg-shaped nuts and crack open by the fire at night. This is the best of the many hickories. Similar ones are black, pignut, shellbark, and mocknut hickory. A taste of the nut tells one from the other.

PECAN

This is also a hickory tree. It is native to the southern river bottoms but is found growing wild in the northeast uplands. You are competing with wild turkeys for this nut.

AMERICAN BEECH

The smooth, gray bark, often carved with names and initials, makes this tree easily identifiable even in winter. Nuts are small and triangular in a hull of spines. Gather in September and October before the squirrels and deer devour them.

PINYON PINE NUTS

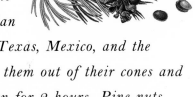

This western pine is a short but handsome tree and one of the oldest southwest Indian foods. It is found in southern Arizona, Texas, Mexico, and the mountains of southern California. Break them out of their cones and preserve them by baking in a 200° F oven for 2 hours. Pine nuts make all foods taste better.

PESTO SAUCE

(Wild nuts enhance any dish, from boiled vegetables to salads, cakes,
ice cream, cookies, and pies, and fish and fowl as well.
Try this pesto sauce using any wild nut.)

4 tablespoons butter

4 cups fresh basil

1 or 2 cloves garlic

½ cup Parmesan cheese

½ cup olive oil

pinch of salt

1 cup of any wild nut

Blend all ingredients in a food processor. Pour sauce over boiled pasta.

WILD NUT PIE

Preheat oven: 350°F

½ cup butter

¾ cup light brown sugar

3 eggs

1 cup light Karo syrup

1 cup chopped wild nuts

1 teaspoon vanilla

pinch of salt

1 9" piecrust

Cream butter and sugar. Beat in eggs, one at a time.

Stir in Karo syrup. Add nuts, vanilla, and salt. Pour into unbaked piecrust. Place on cookie sheet. Bake at 350°F for 45 minutes or until brown. Serve hot or cold.

MAPLE SYRUP WILD NUT CAKE

Preheat oven: 325°F

2 sticks butter

¼ cup cooking oil

1 cup brown sugar

2 cups white sugar

5 eggs, beaten

½ cup self-rising flour

2½ cups plain flour

1 cup milk

1½ cups chopped wild nuts

1 teaspoon vanilla

1 teaspoon maple syrup

Cream the butter, cooking oil, and sugars. Add eggs. Alternately add flours and milk. Add wild nuts, vanilla, and maple syrup. Pour into greased and floured 8"-square cake pan. Bake at 325°F for 1½ hours or until a toothpick emerges clean from cake. Remove from oven. Let cake set for 15 minutes. Turn onto cake rack to cool.

PLANTAINS

• • • •

THE COMMON PLANTAIN (Plantago major) *was brought to North America by Europeans. The Indians called it "white man's foot," for it grows in the midst of civilization. It can be harvested from cracks in city sidewalks, lawns, roadsides, and almost anywhere the earth had been disturbed. The plant is easily recognized by its rosette of leaves that spread out on the ground and stringlike fibers that run in ribs from the foot stalk to the tip of the leaf. Common plantain grows over northeast and north-central North America.*

To serve plantain as a vegetable side dish, pick the smallest and most tender leaves of your backyard plantain. Wash, and simmer in boiling water for 20 minutes. Drain, cut into strips, and serve with butter, salt, and pepper.

Plantain also makes a good addition to the weedy lawn salad (see p. 34).

TEAS

· · · ·

Bring water to a boil and put in wild tea leaves, either fresh or dried, or dried roots. Steep until desired strength is attained. Here are some of my favorites.

LABRADOR TEA

This shrub grows about three feet high. Its woody stems are covered with reddish hairs. It grows over the northern United States and Canada in boggy areas.

SASSAFRAS TEA

The roots of the sassafras make the best tea, but the dried leaves can be used. The tree is recognizable by its three differently shaped leaves: a mitten, an oval, and a three-lobed leaf. Sassafras roots should be dried in the oven or sun to bring out the best flavor.

MINT TEAS

All the many wild mints make tasty teas, but the most savory are the mountain mints, spearmint, pepper-mint, and downy wood mint. They are widespread over North America. The entire mint family has square stems and opposite leaves. You can't miss when you put a square-stemmed plant in your teapot.

STAGHORN SUMAC TEA

This is a small shrub with coarse, soft branches and featherlike leaves. It grows in dry, open soil. The fruits are clustered in a rhomboid and are covered with berrylike seeds. They are dark red and hairy. Boil the fruits in water, and the tea tastes like lemonade.

VIOLETS

• • • •

THE HEART-SHAPED LEAF *of the common blue violet is its hallmark. There are many species of violets, the flowers varying in color from white through yellows to blues and purples. The flowers are delicious and add beauty to fruit salads and all desserts.*

Exquisite Sugared Violets

(This is one of the most beautiful of all the wild foods. Candied violets are sweet scented and exotic. Rose, forsythia, pea, and apple blossoms are other beautiful flowers that can be candied. However, violets are sturdier and easier to handle.)

Preheat oven: 200°F

1 or 2 egg whites

1 box superfine
    granulated sugar

several dozen violets with
    stems

Beat the egg whites until frothy but not stiff. Pour superfine sugar into a bowl. Cover a cookie sheet with waxed paper.

Pick up a violet by the stem and dip into egg white. Dip into sugar until flower is sugared top and bottom. Place on cookie sheet. Using a toothpick, straighten the petals.

Repeat until all violets are dipped. Leave stems as handles to help you remove flowers from paper when done.

Place in oven for about 40 minutes or until sugar is crystallized. It turns frosty white. While the violets are cooking, tear off another piece of waxed paper.

When sugar is crystallized, lift flowers off cookie sheet with spatula, tweezers, or fingers, and place on second sheet of waxed paper.

If the flowers look wet and glisteny, sprinkle with more sugar and return to oven.

Cool for about an hour. Cut off stems and store flowers in airtight box. Place waxed paper between layers. Sugared violets will keep in this manner for a year or more.

CANADA VIOLET SOUP

(This wild yellow violet has more vitamins C and A than spinach.)

2 tablespoons butter

4 cups Canada violet leaves

1 tablespoon chopped onion

1½ cups water

2 bouillon cubes

salt

pepper

Melt butter in skillet. Add Canada violet leaves and onion. Cover and simmer for 10 minutes. Add water and bouillon cubes. Heat until they dissolve. Add salt and pepper to taste.

WOOD SORRELS

THE CLOVERLIKE LEAVES *of the lemon-flavored oxalis, better known as wood sorrel or sour grass, are easy to recognize. There are nine species in the United States and Canada. Most flowers are yellow, although some species are gray, white, or pink-red. The most common is the yellow creeping wood sorrel. A bite of a sorrel leaf will verify its identity: The taste is wonderfully sour and lemony. All wood sorrels are delicious.*

Sorrel Broth

4 cups sorrel (leaves, stems, and flowers; save some for garnish)

1 teaspoon butter

5 cups water and 5 chicken bouillon cubes, or 5 cups chicken broth

4 egg yolks

2 cups light cream

Sauté sorrel in the butter until wilted. Set aside. Bring chicken broth to a boil. (If using bouillon cubes, pour water into saucepan and bring to a boil. Add bouillon cubes and stir until dissolved.) In small bowl, lightly beat together egg yolks and cream.

Remove broth from heat. Add egg mixture, stirring with a whisk. Return to heat and cook over very low heat until slightly thickened, stirring constantly. Do not allow to boil. Remove from heat, add sorrel, and serve hot. Decorate with fresh sorrel leaves and flowers. Also excellent icy cold.

Squash and Sorrel

Add sorrel to yellow squash just before you remove cooked squash from heat.

BUILD A SORREL SANDWICH

2 slices of bread of your
    choice
butter
mayonnaise

½ cup fresh wood sorrel
crushed corn chips
sardines
sliced cucumbers

Butter bread. Cover one slice with mayonnaise. Sprinkle with sorrel.

Pile on crushed corn chips, sardines, cucumbers, and anything else you like such as peanuts, green olives, or cheese.

INDEX